Why you should be poor

Rethinking Wealth and Happiness

By

Neil Potter

About the author

Neil Potter is not your typical author. He's not a millionaire who's here to tell you how to become one. In fact, he's the guy who realized that less stuff often means more happiness.

With a background in finance that would make your head spin (in a good way), Neil has seen firsthand how the world chases after the shiny allure of wealth. But he also knows that true wealth isn't found in bank accounts; it's found in the moments that make you smile and the people who make your heart sing.

Neil is a firm believer in the power of simplicity and contentment. He's the guy who will convince you that decluttering your life is like finding buried treasure in your own backyard. His writing is as practical as it is humorous, with a sprinkle of wisdom that makes you rethink what it means to be truly rich.

When Neil isn't writing about the joys of being "poor," you'll find him sipping a cup of tea, exploring new hiking trails, or sharing a good laugh with friends and family. Because, for Neil, life is all about the simple pleasures and the riches that money can't buy.

Join Neil on this journey as he challenges the status quo, rethinks wealth and happiness, and helps you discover why you should be "poor" in all the right ways.

Appreciation

Dear Reader,

Congratulations on choosing "Why You Should Be Poor: Rethinking Wealth and Happiness" by Neil Potter. We're thrilled to have you join this journey of rediscovering what it means to be truly rich.

In a world that often measures success by the size of our bank accounts, you've taken a step toward exploring a different path. This book is a testament to your curiosity, your willingness to challenge the norm, and your desire to lead a more meaningful life.

As you flip through these pages, we invite you to reflect on your own values, priorities, and aspirations. Neil's unique perspective, blended with humor and wisdom, will inspire you to reconsider the pursuit of wealth and embrace the riches that come with simplicity, contentment, and purpose.

We appreciate your support as a reader. Your decision to explore this book is a vote for a world where true wealth is measured in joy, connections, and moments that make your heart sing.

Thank you for embarking on this enriching journey with us. We hope this book brings you insights, smiles, and a renewed sense of what it means to be truly rich.

Warm regards,

Neil Potter

Copyright

Copyright © 2023 by Neil Potter

and do not participate in or encourage piracy of copyrighted materials.
Thank you for respecting the hard work of the author

Dedication

To those who choose simplicity over excess,
To the ones who treasure moments over possessions,
To the seekers of true wealth in life's simple pleasures,
To the believers that happiness need not come with a price tag,

This book is dedicated to you.

May these pages inspire you to embrace a life of contentment, purpose, and joy, and may you discover the richness that lies in being "poor" in all the right ways.

With gratitude and admiration,

Neil Potter

Table of contents

Discovering Your True Calling

Chapter 6: Redefining Success

Unconventional Paths to Success

Chapter 7: The Joy of Giving

Finding Happiness Through Giving

Chapter 8: Financial Freedom vs. Material Wealth

Strategies for Financial Independence and Balance

Chapter 9: Embracing the Journey

Living in the Present and Savoring Small Pleasures

Chapter 10: The Path to True Wealth

Reevaluating Our Pursuit of Wealth

Embracing the Journey to True Wealth

Conclusion: The Riches of Being Poor

Embracing a Simpler, More Purposeful Existence

Why You Should Be Poor (But Not Really)

Wise saying from scholars, influential and successful people

The richest people in the world look for and build networks. Everyone else looks for work." — ***Robert Kiyosaki***

"Happiness is not in the mere possession of money; it lies in the joy of achievement, in the thrill of creative effort." — ***Franklin D. Roosevelt***

"The greatest wealth is to live content with little." — ***Plato***

"Success is not the key to happiness. Happiness is the key to success. If you love what you are doing, you will be successful." — ***Albert Schweitzer***

"The ability to simplify means to eliminate the unnecessary so that the necessary may speak." — ***Hans Hofmann***

"Wealth consists not in having great possessions, but in having few wants." — ***Epictetus***

"The more you know, the less you need." — ***Yvon Chouinard***

"The best things in life aren't things." — ***Art Buchwald***

"Money is only a tool. It will take you wherever you wish, but it will not replace you as the driver." — ***Ayn Rand***

"Simplicity is the ultimate sophistication." — ***Leonardo da Vinci***

These quotes reflect the wisdom of those who have contemplated the true nature of wealth and happiness, offering insights that align with the themes of your book.

Introduction

Welcome to a book that's about to turn things upside down, just like that mysterious sock that vanishes in the dryer. In this journey, we're going to explore why you should be poor. And before you grab your pitchforks and start a "stuff appreciation" rally, let's dive in with a pinch of humor and a dash of wisdom.

The Quest for More Stuff: We live in a world that worships stuff. The bigger, the shinier, the better. But what if having more stuff isn't the answer to a better life? What if, just maybe, less is more?

Less Clutter, More Laughter: If you've ever tried to find your phone under a mountain of things on your desk, you know the pain of clutter. Being poor (in stuff, mind you) can lead to a clutter-free existence. So, you'll find your phone in seconds, not hours.

Money, Money, Money: Being poor means you can be rich in money that's not spent on stuff. That's like having a secret savings account for spontaneous adventures.

The Joy of Contentment: Contentment is the real MVP. Being poor in wanting more can lead to a happier, more Zen-like life. You're no longer chasing the "next big thing."

The Art of Letting Go: Ever try decluttering? It's like a treasure hunt where you find old photos, lost keys, and that one sock. It's also strangely liberating.

The Simplicity Code: Simplicity is the ultimate sophistication, they say. Being poor in complications can simplify your life in the best way possible.

So, why should we be poor? Because sometimes, less really is more. It's about finding richness in simplicity, contentment in the everyday, and laughter in the unlikeliest places. This book is your guide to a "poor" life that's secretly a goldmine. So, fasten your seatbelt; we're about to embark on an adventure where the road less cluttered leads to true riches.

The Paradox of Wealth

The Paradox of Wealth refers to the notion that while material wealth can provide comfort and security, it often does not guarantee happiness or fulfillment. This concept highlights several important points:

Diminishing Returns:

Research in psychology and economics has shown that beyond a certain point, increased wealth does not significantly contribute to increased happiness. Once basic needs are met, additional wealth may have diminishing returns in terms of life satisfaction.

Materialism vs. Well-being:

The pursuit of material possessions and wealth can lead to materialism, where individuals prioritize material goods over experiences, relationships, and personal well-being. This can result in a sense of emptiness and dissatisfaction.

Psychological Factors:

Happiness and well-being are influenced by a variety of psychological factors, such as mindset, gratitude, and social connections, which are not solely dependent on wealth.

Social Comparison:

People often engage in social comparison, measuring their success and happiness relative to others. This can lead to a perpetual cycle of striving for more wealth in order to keep up with or surpass others, which may not lead to greater happiness.

Time and Stress:

The pursuit of wealth can consume significant time and energy, leading to high stress levels, long work hours, and a reduced quality of life. This can result in a paradox where the pursuit of wealth undermines the very well-being it aims to enhance.

Values and Meaning:

True fulfillment often comes from pursuing one's values and finding meaning in life. The relentless pursuit of wealth, if not aligned with personal values and a sense of purpose, can lead to a sense of hollowness.

Economic Security vs. Happiness:

While economic security is important for overall well-being, excessive focus on accumulating wealth at the expense of other life domains can lead to imbalances that negatively impact happiness.

In essence, the Paradox of Wealth suggests that while wealth can provide opportunities and security, it is not a direct path to happiness and well-being. Achieving a balance between financial stability and other aspects of life, such as relationships, personal growth, and community involvement, is essential for a more holistic and fulfilling existence.

Society's obsession with wealth and the pursuit of material success.

Society's obsession with wealth and the relentless pursuit of material success are deeply ingrained aspects of modern culture. This obsession manifests in various ways and has both positive and negative consequences:

Positive Aspects:

1. Motivation and Innovation:

The pursuit of wealth can drive individuals and businesses to innovate, create new products, and improve existing ones. This can lead to technological advancements and economic growth.

2. Economic Prosperity:

A society focused on economic success often experiences overall prosperity, with opportunities for employment and increased living standards for many.

3. **Charitable Giving:**

Some individuals who accumulate substantial wealth use it for philanthropic purposes, contributing to important social causes, such as education, healthcare, and poverty alleviation.

Negative Aspects:

1. **Materialism:**

The relentless pursuit of wealth can lead to materialism, where possessions and conspicuous consumption become the primary sources of personal value and identity.

2. **Stress and Anxiety:**

The pressure to attain wealth and maintain a certain lifestyle can lead to high levels of stress and anxiety, as individuals constantly strive for more and fear losing what they have.

3. **Income Inequality:**

The pursuit of wealth can exacerbate income inequality within society, with a small percentage of the population amassing significant resources while many struggle to make ends meet.

4. **Loss of Values:**

The focus on material success can sometimes lead to a loss of core values, such as compassion, empathy, and a sense of community, as individuals prioritize personal gain above all else.

5. **Environmental Impact:**

The pursuit of wealth often involves resource exploitation and environmental degradation, contributing to issues like climate change and habitat destruction.

6. **Shallow Relationships:**

People consumed by the pursuit of wealth may prioritize work and personal success over meaningful relationships, potentially leading to loneliness and social disconnection.

7. **Mental Health Issues:**

The pressure to achieve societal standards of success can contribute to mental health issues, including depression and burnout.

In summary, society's obsession with wealth and material success is a complex phenomenon with both positive and negative consequences. While it can drive progress and innovation, it also has the potential to erode values, cause stress, and exacerbate social and environmental problems. Achieving a balanced approach that values well-being, sustainability, and meaningful relationships alongside financial success is a significant challenge facing modern societies.

Redefining our notions of wealth

In the midst of a world ceaselessly chasing financial riches and unrestrained prosperity, there lies a captivating paradox—one that challenges the very essence of our conventional beliefs about wealth and fulfillment where we dare to contemplate an extraordinary notion: that the path to a profoundly fulfilling life might begin by embracing, or at least reimagining, the virtues of modesty and simplicity.

The Great Pursuit

Our lives are often framed by a relentless chase for affluence. We are taught that wealth, in its most tangible form, is the ultimate harbinger of happiness. And so, we embark on a quest, striving for that larger house, that shinier car, or that bloated bank account. Yet, have we ever paused to ponder whether this quest leads us closer to the contentment we seek, or if it instead blinds us to the beauty of the present moment?

The Mirage of Materialism

Materialism, that unrelenting pursuit of possessions, has woven an enchanting but deceptive web around us. It whispers promises of joy and fulfillment with each new acquisition. Yet, if we stop to listen more closely, we might hear the faint echoes of disillusionment and emptiness that follow.

Wealth Beyond Measure

What if wealth were not merely a numeric reflection of one's financial assets? What if it encompassed the immeasurable beauty of a starry night, the priceless laughter of a child, and the boundless love of a loyal friend? What if it extended to the wealth of experiences, of kind gestures, and of shared moments that enrich the human spirit?

The Hidden Bounty of Less

In the pursuit of more, we often overlook the profound riches of less. By shedding the burdens of consumerism and material excess, we may unlock a treasure trove of contentment that has eluded us in our relentless chase for wealth.

The Odyssey Ahead

As we journey deeper into this unconventional terrain, we'll encounter individuals who have chosen to redefine their relationship with wealth and have discovered a more authentic and fulfilling existence in the process. Together, we'll explore the notion that the road to genuine prosperity may very well lie in shedding the conventional definitions of wealth and embracing a life imbued with simplicity, mindfulness, and purpose.

Dear reader, if you've ever wondered whether there might be a more profound and unconventional path to fulfillment, join us on this expedition. Let us embark on a journey of discovery and introspection, as we contemplate the paradox that being "poor" in the traditional sense might just lead us to an unparalleled richness of life.

Chapter 1: The Illusion of Wealth

In our modern world, it's easy to fall under the spell of material wealth. We're bombarded daily with images of opulence and luxury, making it seem like the pursuit of wealth is the ultimate path to happiness and success. But as we navigate the complexities of our lives, it's crucial to recognize the illusion that often accompanies the accumulation of wealth.

The Mirage of Happiness

Picture this: a brand-new car, the latest smartphone, a designer wardrobe – these symbols of affluence can make us feel on top of the world, if only for a moment. But the thrill tends to fade quickly, leaving us chasing the next purchase, the next upgrade, and the next source of momentary pleasure. It's the illusion of wealth – the belief that more possessions will lead to lasting happiness.

The Relentless Pursuit

In the quest for material wealth, we often find ourselves on a treadmill of constant striving. It's as if we're running a race with no finish line. The more we earn, the more we desire, creating a cycle of never-ending pursuit. Psychologists call it the "hedonic treadmill." It's a reminder that our desires can expand infinitely, leaving us perpetually dissatisfied.

The Burden of Expectation

Living under the shadow of material wealth can also bring a heavy burden of expectation. We feel pressure to maintain appearances, to keep up with the Joneses, and to continually outdo ourselves. This pressure can lead to stress, anxiety, and a sense of inadequacy.

The True Wealth Within

So, what's the way out of this illusion? It starts with redefining our notions of wealth. True wealth isn't just about what's in your bank account or your collection of possessions. It's about the quality of your experiences, the richness of your relationships, and the sense of purpose you find in your life.

An Enlightened Path

In this modern age, we have the opportunity to break free from the illusion of wealth. We can choose to value experiences over things, relationships over status, and purpose over possessions. It's a shift in perspective that can lead to a life of greater contentment and fulfillment.

As we journey forward, remember that the pursuit of wealth is not inherently wrong.

It's the illusion that more is always better that we must dispel. By understanding the illusion and choosing a path that aligns with our true values, we can find genuine wealth in the simplicity, mindfulness, and purpose that modern life often obscures.

The cost of chasing wealth

In our fast-paced, modern lives, the pursuit of wealth is a common goal. We see images of success all around us – people with big houses, fancy cars, and lavish vacations. It's natural to want a comfortable life, but let's take a closer look at how the relentless chase for wealth can come at a cost: stress, anxiety, and a sense of emptiness.

The Pressure to Keep Up

Imagine scrolling through your social media feed. You see friends posting about their new gadgets, their luxurious vacations, or their latest shopping sprees. It's easy to start feeling like you need those things too. You might think, "If they have it, why shouldn't I?" This pressure to keep up with others can create stress.

The Burden of Debt

To afford the things we see others enjoying, we might turn to credit cards or loans. These debts can pile up quickly, leading to financial stress. You find yourself constantly worrying about bills, interest rates, and the pressure to make ends meet.

The Never-Ending Race

You might have a well-paying job, but it often feels like you're running on a never-ending treadmill. The pursuit of wealth can lead to longer work hours, more responsibilities, and less time for yourself and your loved ones. The constant pressure to earn more can lead to anxiety and burnout.

The Elusive Sense of Fulfillment

Now, let's talk about that sense of emptiness. You've worked hard, earned a good income, and acquired many things, but somehow, you still feel unsatisfied. You realize that the possessions you've accumulated haven't brought the lasting happiness you expected.

The Impact on Mental Health

Stress and anxiety can take a toll on your mental health. You might find it hard to sleep, relax, or enjoy simple pleasures. Your mind is constantly racing, thinking about money, work, and what you should achieve next.

Breaking the Cycle

It's important to pause and reflect. Are you truly happy with the path you're on? Is the pursuit of wealth worth the stress and anxiety it brings? Many people are reevaluating their priorities and finding that a simpler, more balanced life leads to greater fulfillment.

Consider this: What if wealth isn't just about money and possessions? What if it's also about your well-being, your relationships, and your sense of purpose? In the chapters ahead, we'll explore how you can find a more balanced and fulfilling life by redefining your notions of wealth and success.

Remember, you're not alone in feeling the pressure to chase wealth, but you have the power to make choices that prioritize your happiness and well-being above all else.

The Pursuit of Wealth

Let's dive into the lives of real people who achieved remarkable financial success but discovered it didn't bring the happiness they thought it would. Their stories are a reflection of our modern world, where wealth is often seen as the ultimate goal.

Meet Sarah: The CEO

Sarah climbed the corporate ladder with determination. She became the CEO of a major tech company, earning a substantial salary. She had a luxurious home, a collection of high-end cars, and could afford lavish vacations. Yet, with all her wealth and success, she often found herself working late into the night, missing family gatherings, and feeling disconnected from her loved ones. The more she gained in wealth, the more she lost in precious moments and personal happiness.

John: The Investment Whiz

John had a knack for investments. He made brilliant financial choices and amassed a fortune. His bank account was impressive, but as he reached the pinnacle of wealth, he realized something was missing. He lacked a sense of purpose. Without a deeper reason for his financial pursuits, John found his life lacked meaning. The thrill of earning more money had faded, leaving an emptiness he couldn't ignore.

Linda: The Entrepreneur

Linda was an entrepreneur with multiple successful businesses. She had a luxurious lifestyle, traveled the world, and enjoyed the finest things money could buy. Yet, beneath the façade of prosperity, she struggled with stress and anxiety. Her constant pursuit of wealth had taken a toll on her well-being. Linda longed for peace of mind and a simpler, less stressful life.

What We Can Learn

These stories remind us that financial success alone isn't a guaranteed path to happiness. In our modern lives, it's easy to get caught up in the pursuit of wealth and overlook the importance of balance, purpose, and personal well-being.

Consider this: What if true wealth isn't just about the money in your bank account, but also about the quality of your relationships, your sense of purpose, and your overall contentment? These stories show us that redefining our notions of wealth and success can lead to a more fulfilling and balanced life.

In the chapters ahead, we'll explore how you can find a harmonious balance between financial success and personal happiness. It's a journey that many are embarking on in our modern world, seeking a life where wealth serves as a means to an end, rather than the end itself.

Chapter 2: The Cost of Consumerism

In our modern lives, consumerism is a powerful force. It encourages us to buy, spend, and accumulate more and more. But, there's a cost to this way of living, and it affects us in very personal ways.

The Shopping Frenzy

Imagine going to a mall or shopping online. It's easy to get caught up in the excitement of buying new things. But, as we accumulate more stuff, we often spend money we don't have. This leads to something called "consumer debt."

The Debt Dilemma

Consumer debt is like a cloud that hangs over us. It's the money we owe for all the things we bought but couldn't pay for right away. Credit cards, loans, and installment plans make it tempting to overspend. But, in the end, we pay more because of interest, and it can cause a lot of stress.

The Work-Life Struggle

To afford our shopping habits, many of us end up working longer hours or taking on extra jobs. We're constantly chasing after the next paycheck to cover our expenses. This leaves less time for our families, hobbies, and relaxation, leading to a work-life imbalance.

Environmental Impact

Consumerism isn't just costly for us personally; it also has a big impact on the planet. Many of the things we buy are produced using energy and resources that harm the environment. From single-use plastics to fast fashion, our choices contribute to pollution and climate change.

Reevaluating Our Priorities

In the midst of consumerism, it's essential to take a step back and ask ourselves if this is the life we want. Is the pursuit of more stuff worth the financial stress, the time away from loved ones, and the damage to our planet?

Choosing a Different Path

In the chapters ahead, we'll explore how you can make choices that prioritize your well-being and the environment. It's about finding a balance between enjoying what you have and making mindful decisions about what you truly need.

Remember, you have the power to shape your relationship with consumerism. By understanding the costs it can bring and making intentional choices, you can lead a more fulfilling and sustainable life in our modern world.

The Consumer Culture Conundrum

In our fast-paced, modern lives, consumer culture is all around us. We're constantly encouraged to buy more, have more, and indulge in the latest trends. But there are hidden costs to this culture that affect our daily lives and the world around us.

The Allure of Consumerism

Imagine a day in your life. You wake up to your smartphone's alarm, check social media on your tablet, and brew coffee with a single-use pod machine. Throughout the day, you use countless products, from disposable water bottles to fast fashion clothes. Consumer culture makes it easy to acquire these things, but it also brings consequences.

Debt: The Silent Strain

One of the most common consequences of consumer culture is debt. Buying on credit or taking out loans to afford the latest gadgets or fashion trends can lead to financial stress. It's like a heavy backpack you have to carry, with interest rates that make it harder to pay off.

Overwork and Burnout

Consumer culture often encourages us to work harder and longer to afford more things. We take on extra hours or side gigs to keep up with the latest purchases. This relentless pace can lead to overwork and burnout, affecting our mental and physical health.

Environmental Impact: A Planet in Peril

Think about all the products you use in a single day. Many of them are made from finite resources and contribute to pollution and waste. The environmental impact of our consumer habits is substantial, from single-use plastics clogging our oceans to carbon emissions from manufacturing.

The Quest for Balance

Consumer culture can be like a never-ending race, always pushing us to want more. But it's essential to pause and ask ourselves if this is the life we truly want. Are the things we buy worth the environmental toll and the stress they bring? Can we find happiness in simpler, more sustainable choices?
Remember, you have the power to shape your relationship with consumer culture. By understanding the costs it can bring and making intentional choices, you can lead a more fulfilling and sustainable life.

Embracing a More Fulfilling Path

In our consumer-driven world, there's a different way to live – one that's more sustainable and fulfilling. This chapter explores alternatives to excessive consumption, helping you discover a more meaningful life.

The Joy of Experiences

Instead of buying more things, consider investing in experiences. Go on adventures, travel to new places, or learn a new skill. These moments often bring greater joy and lasting memories than material possessions.

The Art of Minimalism

Minimalism is about simplifying your life by owning fewer things. It's not about having nothing; it's about having what truly adds value. By decluttering and letting go of excess stuff, you can create a more peaceful and organized living space.

Mindful Consumption

When you do need to buy something, be mindful about it. Ask yourself if it's something you genuinely need or if it's just a passing want. Look for products that are built to last and have a smaller environmental footprint.

Quality Over Quantity

Instead of buying lots of cheap items, consider investing in quality products that will last longer. They may cost more upfront, but they often save you money in the long run and reduce waste.

Giving and Sharing

Find joy in giving and sharing with others. Whether it's donating to a cause you care about, volunteering your time, or sharing resources with friends and neighbors, these acts of kindness can be incredibly fulfilling.

Nature's Beauty

Connect with nature. Spending time outdoors, whether it's hiking, gardening, or simply going for a walk, can be rejuvenating. It reminds us of the beauty of the world around us and our responsibility to protect it.

The Power of Contentment

Practice gratitude and contentment. Instead of always wanting more, take time to appreciate what you have. Gratitude can lead to a sense of fulfillment that goes beyond material possessions.

Community and Relationships

Invest in your relationships. Spend quality time with family and friends. Building strong connections can provide a deep sense of purpose and happiness.

The Journey Ahead

Choosing a more sustainable and meaningful life doesn't mean you have to give up everything. It's about finding a balance that works for you.

Remember, you have the power to shape your life in a way that aligns with your values and brings you true fulfillment in our modern and consumer-focused society.

Chapter 3: The Value of Simplicity

In our fast-paced, complex world, simplicity can be a beacon of light. This chapter explores the value of simplicity and how it can bring clarity, peace, and meaning to our modern lives.

Less Is More

Simplicity is the idea that less can be more. It's about focusing on what truly matters and letting go of unnecessary complexity. In our everyday lives, it means decluttering our physical and mental spaces.

Clarity in Chaos

In a world filled with constant information and distractions, simplicity offers clarity. It's like cleaning the dust off a window, allowing you to see the world outside more clearly. By simplifying your surroundings and your schedule, you can reduce stress and anxiety.

Peaceful Living

Simplicity can lead to a sense of peace. Imagine coming home to a tidy, uncluttered space. It's easier to relax and unwind when your environment is simple and serene. This peace extends to your mind, helping you find inner calm amidst life's challenges.

Meaningful Connections

When we simplify our lives, we make more time for what truly matters. This includes spending quality moments with loved ones, pursuing our passions, and finding meaning in our daily activities. Simplicity can lead to more fulfilling relationships and a deeper sense of purpose.

The Power of Mindfulness

Mindfulness is about being present in the moment. Simplicity encourages mindfulness by helping us appreciate the little things in life. Whether it's savoring a home-cooked meal or enjoying a walk in nature, simplicity reminds us to be fully present.

Choosing Simplicity

Simplicity doesn't mean giving up everything or living in a bare room. It's about making intentional choices that align with your values and bring you joy. It's about finding balance in a world that often pushes us to do more and have more.

The Journey Ahead

In the chapters to come, we'll delve deeper into the practical ways you can embrace simplicity in your life. We'll explore decluttering techniques, time management strategies, and mindfulness practices that can help you simplify and find greater fulfillment in our modern world.

Remember, simplicity is a powerful tool that can enhance your well-being and bring more meaning to your life. It's a journey of self-discovery and intentional living, and it starts with a single step toward a simpler, more fulfilling life.

Simplifying Your Life

Now that we understand the benefits of simplicity and minimalism, let's dive into some practical steps you can take to simplify your life and reduce material possessions in our modern world.

Declutter with Purpose

Start by decluttering your space. Go through your belongings and ask yourself, "Does this add value to my life?" If the answer is no, consider letting it go. This can be clothes you no longer wear, gadgets you no longer use, or knick-knacks collecting dust.

One In, One Out Rule

To maintain a clutter-free environment, adopt the "one in, one out" rule. When you bring in a new item, commit to letting go of something you already have. This ensures that your possessions stay manageable.

Digital Declutter

Our digital lives can be cluttered too. Go through your digital files, emails, and apps. Delete what you no longer need and organize your digital space for efficiency. This will reduce digital stress.

Practice Mindful Consumption

Before making a purchase, pause and ask yourself if it's something you truly need or if it's just a fleeting want. Consider the impact of your choices on your finances and the environment.

Quality Over Quantity

Invest in high-quality items that are built to last rather than buying cheap, disposable products. Quality items often save you money in the long run and reduce waste.

Create Designated Spaces

Designate specific spaces for your belongings. When everything has its place, it's easier to keep things organized and avoid unnecessary clutter.

Streamline Your Wardrobe

Consider a minimalist wardrobe. Keep only the clothing you love and wear regularly. A smaller, curated wardrobe can make getting dressed simpler and more enjoyable.

Let Go Gradually

Simplifying doesn't mean you have to declutter everything at once. Take your time and let go of possessions gradually. It's a journey, not a race.

Practice Gratitude

Cultivate gratitude for what you have. Regularly remind yourself of the value in your life. Gratitude can help you find contentment and reduce the desire for more stuff.

Digital Detox

Periodically disconnect from technology. Unplug from screens and spend time in the physical world. This break can help clear your mind and reduce digital overwhelm.

Share and Donate

Consider sharing or donating items you no longer need. Someone else might find value in what you're no longer using.

Stay Committed

Simplicity is a lifestyle choice. Stay committed to your journey of simplification, and regularly revisit your possessions to ensure they align with your values and priorities.

By incorporating these practical tips into your life, you can simplify your surroundings, reduce material possessions, and experience the freedom and contentment that simplicity brings to our modern world.

Chapter 4: The Power of Relationships

In our fast-paced, technology-driven world, the value of relationships cannot be overstated. This chapter explores the profound impact that connections with others have on our modern and personal lives.

The Digital Age Dilemma

In the digital age, we're more connected than ever, but sometimes it feels like we're drifting apart. We have online friends, but face-to-face conversations become rarer. It's time to recognize the power of real, meaningful relationships.

The Joy of Connection

Think about the people in your life who bring you joy and support. It could be family, friends, or mentors. These connections enrich our lives, offering emotional support, laughter, and shared experiences.

Shared Moments and Memories

Our most cherished moments often involve the people we care about. Whether it's celebrating a birthday, sharing a meal, or simply enjoying a conversation, these moments create lasting memories.

Facing Life's Challenges Together

Life isn't always smooth sailing. During tough times, our relationships provide a safety net. Friends and family can offer emotional support, helping us navigate challenges with resilience.

Professional Networks

Relationships aren't limited to personal life. In our careers, professional networks open doors to opportunities, collaboration, and personal growth. The people we know can shape our success.

Quality Over Quantity

It's not about having a vast number of connections. Quality matters more than quantity. Meaningful relationships involve trust, empathy, and mutual respect.

Making Time for Connections

In our busy lives, it's crucial to prioritize relationships. Set aside time for loved ones, pick up the phone for a chat, or arrange face-to-face meetings. These efforts nurture the bonds that matter most.

Connection in the Digital Age

While technology can sometimes hinder our connections, it can also facilitate them. Reach out to distant friends or family through video calls or social media to bridge geographical gaps.

The Power of Listening

Listening is a key component of strong relationships. Truly hearing what someone has to say fosters understanding and empathy. Practice active listening in your conversations.

Choosing Empathy

Empathy is the ability to understand and share the feelings of others. Cultivate empathy in your relationships, and you'll deepen your connections and strengthen your bonds.

The Journey Ahead

As we navigate our modern lives, let's remember that the power of relationships can bring us fulfillment, support, and a sense of belonging. In the chapters to come, we'll explore ways to nurture and strengthen these vital connections.

Our relationships are like the threads that weave the fabric of our lives. By valuing and tending to these threads, we can create a tapestry of happiness and meaning that enriches our journey in this digital age.

The Strength of Connections

In our modern lives, the value of relationships is immeasurable. This chapter delves into the profound impact that our connections with others have on our personal and everyday life.

Modern Loneliness

In today's fast-paced world, we may have hundreds of online friends, but we often feel a sense of loneliness. The digital age has brought us closer virtually but sometimes farther apart in the real world. It's time to rediscover the true power of genuine relationships.

Shared Joy and Support

Think about the people who make your life brighter—the friends, family, or colleagues who lend a helping hand or share a heartfelt laugh. These connections bring us joy, emotional support, and a sense of belonging.

Memories That Bind

Our most cherished memories are often intertwined with the people we care about. Whether it's celebrating an achievement, sharing a meal, or simply chatting on the porch, these moments become lasting memories we hold dear.

Facing Life Together

Life can be a bumpy ride. During tough times, our relationships act as a safety net. Friends and family provide emotional support, helping us weather life's storms with resilience.

Building Bridges in Careers

Connections aren't confined to our personal lives. In our careers, professional networks open doors to opportunities, collaborations, and personal growth. The people we know can shape our success.

Quality Over Quantity

It's not about collecting a vast number of contacts. What truly matters is the quality of our relationships. Meaningful connections are built on trust, empathy, and mutual respect.

Prioritizing Relationships

In our hectic lives, it's essential to prioritize our relationships. Carve out time for loved ones, pick up the phone for a heartfelt conversation, or arrange meet-ups. These efforts nurture the bonds that matter most.

Balancing the Digital World

While technology can sometimes hinder our connections, it can also facilitate them. Use digital tools to stay in touch with distant friends or family, bridging geographical gaps.

The Gift of Listening

Listening is a cornerstone of strong relationships. Truly hearing what someone has to say fosters understanding and empathy. Practice active listening to enrich your interactions.

Cultivating Empathy

Empathy, the ability to understand and share others' feelings, is a cornerstone of strong connections. Nurture empathy in your relationships, and you'll deepen your connections and fortify your bonds.

The Journey Ahead

As we navigate our modern lives, let's never underestimate the power of relationships to bring us fulfillment, support, and a sense of belonging. In the chapters ahead, we'll explore ways to nurture and strengthen these vital connections.

Our relationships are the threads that weave the tapestry of our lives. By treasuring and tending to these threads, we can create a rich and colorful life that enriches our journey in this digital age.

Prioritizing Relationships

In our modern world, stories of people who prioritize relationships over wealth inspire us to rethink our priorities and live richer, more fulfilling lives. Here are a few of these real-life stories:

Sarah: The Family First Advocate

Sarah had a high-paying job and a life filled with material comforts. But she realized that she hardly spent time with her family. She made a bold decision to leave her demanding job and opt for a simpler lifestyle. Today, she runs a small family business and has more time to be with her loved ones. Her relationships have deepened, and she describes her life as richer and more meaningful than ever.

John: The Giving Guru

John was a successful entrepreneur who accumulated wealth over the years. But he felt something was missing. He decided to use his resources to make a difference in the lives of others. He founded a nonprofit organization that helps underprivileged children access education. John says that the joy of giving and the connections he's made through his charitable work have enriched his life beyond measure.

Linda: The Traveling Bond Builder

Linda was a frequent traveler, exploring exotic destinations and staying in luxury resorts. Yet, she often felt lonely on her journeys. She decided to change her approach and began traveling with friends and family. These shared adventures not only strengthened her relationships but also brought a richness to her life that no amount of luxury could provide.

Mark: The Time Millionaire

Mark was a workaholic who achieved financial success but was missing out on life's precious moments. He decided to rebalance his priorities. He reduced his work hours and started spending more time with his children, attending their school events and family outings. Mark now feels like a "time millionaire," cherishing the moments he spends with his loved ones.

Grace: The Community Connector

Grace lived in a bustling city but often felt disconnected from her neighbors. She started organizing neighborhood gatherings and events to bring people together. As a result, she formed strong bonds with her community and found a sense of belonging that money couldn't buy. Her life is now filled with friendships and a vibrant sense of community.

These stories remind us that prioritizing relationships can lead to richer, more fulfilling lives. In our modern world, where the pursuit of wealth often takes center stage, these individuals found true wealth in the connections they fostered with others. Their experiences inspire us to seek balance and meaning through our own relationships.

In our modern lives, finding and following your passion and purpose can lead to a deeply fulfilling journey. This chapter explores the significance of pursuing what truly matters to you.

Modern Dilemma

Many of us spend our days on autopilot, going through the motions of daily life. We work to pay the bills, but something may be missing—a sense of passion and purpose that makes us feel truly alive.

Discovering Passion

Passion is that spark that ignites your soul. It's what you love to do, the thing that makes your heart race. In our modern world, discovering your passion might take time, but it's worth the search.

Living with Purpose

Purpose is the "why" behind what you do. It's about making a positive impact, whether on your own life, the lives of others, or the world. Living with purpose gives meaning to your actions.

Balancing Passion and Purpose

Your passion and purpose are like two puzzle pieces that fit together. When you find what you're passionate about and align it with your sense of purpose, you create a powerful force that drives you forward.

Modern Opportunities

In today's digital age, opportunities to explore your passions and live with purpose are more accessible than ever. You can turn your hobbies into side gigs, volunteer for causes you care about, or create content that inspires others.

Overcoming Obstacles

Pursuing passion and purpose isn't always easy. There will be challenges and setbacks along the way. But these obstacles can be stepping stones to growth and fulfillment.

Remember, your passion and purpose are waiting to be discovered. They hold the keys to a life that's not only successful but also deeply fulfilling. As you embark on this journey, you'll find that pursuing what truly matters can lead to a richer and more satisfying life.

The Significance of Passion and Purpose

In our fast-paced, modern lives, the pursuit of passion and purpose holds profound importance. This chapter explores why discovering and following your passions can transform your life.

The Modern Quandary

Many of us live in a kind of autopilot mode, where each day feels routine and predictable. We work to make ends meet, but something seems amiss—a longing for a deeper sense of meaning and fulfillment.

The Power of Passion

Passion is the fire within you, the thing that sets your soul on fire. It's what you love to do, the activity that brings you joy and excitement. In our modern world, uncovering your passion might take time, but its impact can be life-changing.

Fueling Your Journey

Imagine passion as your engine and purpose as your map. When you combine them, you embark on a journey that feels authentic and fulfilling. Your passion fuels your drive, while your purpose guides your path.

Modern Avenues

In our digital age, opportunities to explore your passions and live with purpose are abundant. You can turn your interests into side projects, engage in volunteer work that aligns with your values, or share your talents with a global audience online.

Overcoming Obstacles

Pursuing passion and purpose may come with challenges and setbacks, but these are part of the journey. They teach you resilience and help you appreciate the rewards even more.

The Path Ahead

In the chapters to come, we'll delve deeper into how you can uncover your passions and align them with your sense of purpose in our modern world. We'll offer practical advice and stories to inspire and guide you on your quest for a more meaningful life.

Remember, your passions and purpose are like treasure waiting to be discovered. They are the keys to a life that's not just successful but deeply satisfying. As you embark on this journey, you'll find that pursuing what truly matters can lead to a richer and more fulfilling life in our modern age.

Discovering Your True Calling

In our modern and busy lives, finding your true calling can be a transformative journey. This chapter offers guidance on how to identify and pursue your life's purpose.

The Search for Meaning

Many of us wonder, "What's my purpose?" It's a question that can lead to a richer, more fulfilling life. But how do you begin the search for your true calling?

Exploring Passions

Start by exploring your passions. What activities make your heart sing? What do you lose track of time doing? Your passions often hold clues to your true calling.

Unearth Your Strengths

Take stock of your strengths and talents. What comes naturally to you? Your unique abilities can point you in the direction of your life's purpose.

Consider Your Values

Reflect on your values. What principles and causes do you deeply care about? Aligning your true calling with your values can bring profound fulfillment.

Seek Inspiration

Look for inspiration in the lives of others. Read books, watch documentaries, or listen to podcasts about people who've discovered their true callings. Their journeys may spark ideas for your own path.

Experiment and Explore

Don't be afraid to try new things. Experiment with different activities, volunteer for causes, or take on side projects. This hands-on approach can help you uncover your true calling.

Listen to Your Inner Voice

Pay attention to your intuition. Sometimes, your inner voice knows what's right for you. Tune in to your instincts—they can lead you toward your purpose.

Learn from Failures

Embrace failures as opportunities for growth. Sometimes, discovering your true calling involves a few wrong turns. Learn from these experiences and keep moving forward.

Seek Guidance

Consider seeking guidance from mentors, counselors, or coaches. They can provide valuable insights and support as you navigate your path.

The Journey Ahead

Remember, the pursuit of your life's purpose is a dynamic and evolving process. It's about listening to your heart and taking steps, no matter how small, toward a more meaningful life in our modern world.

Chapter 6: Redefining Success

In our modern world, success is often measured by external standards—wealth, status, and achievements. But it's time to challenge these conventional definitions and create your own metrics for success.

The Standard Definition

Society often tells us that success means a big paycheck, a prestigious job title, or a fancy car. But these external markers don't always lead to fulfillment.

What Does Success Mean to You?

Start by asking yourself, "What does success look like in my life?" Success is deeply personal. It could mean having time to spend with loved ones, pursuing a passion, or contributing to a cause you care about.

Measuring Your Happiness

Think about what truly makes you happy. Is it a sense of purpose, strong relationships, or the freedom to do what you love? These are valid metrics for success.

Embracing Individuality

Your path to success is unique. It doesn't have to match anyone else's. Don't be afraid to go against the grain and define success on your terms.

Balancing Your Priorities

Consider what truly matters to you. Is it more time with family? Pursuing a creative endeavor? Balancing your priorities can redefine your sense of success.

Celebrating Small Wins

Success isn't always about big achievements. Celebrate the small wins along the way. They are stepping stones on your journey.

Embracing Failure

Don't fear failure. It's a part of every success story. Learn from your setbacks and keep moving forward.

Living Authentically

Redefining success is about living authentically. It's about aligning your actions with your values and passions.

The Journey Ahead

In the chapters that follow, we'll delve deeper into how you can create your own metrics for success and lead a more meaningful life. Remember, success isn't one-size-fits-all. It's about embracing your uniqueness and defining what truly matters to you in our modern world.

Unconventional Paths to Success

In our modern lives, success stories often follow unexpected routes. This chapter explores inspiring tales of individuals who found both success and happiness through unconventional paths.

Lena: The Artistic Explorer

Lena spent years in a corporate job, but her true passion was art. She decided to take a leap of faith, leaving her stable career to become a full-time artist. Her unconventional path led her to create beautiful works of art that brought joy to people's lives, and she found success doing what she loved most.

David: The Social Entrepreneur

David was a tech-savvy engineer, but he couldn't ignore the world's social and environmental problems. He started a nonprofit organization that combined technology with social impact. His unconventional approach not only addressed critical issues but also inspired others to follow in his footsteps.

Emma: The Nomadic Writer

Emma was stuck in a 9-to-5 job that left her unfulfilled. She dreamed of traveling and writing about her adventures. She took a risk, quit her job, and began her journey as a nomadic writer. Through her travel blogs and books, she not only explored the world but also found success and happiness in sharing her experiences.

Marcus: The Late Bloomer

Marcus pursued a traditional career for most of his life. It wasn't until his late 40s that he discovered his true calling in teaching. He went back to school to become an educator, and his unconventional journey led him to inspire and educate generations of students, proving that it's never too late to find success in something you're passionate about.

Lucy: The Volunteer Extraordinaire

Lucy had a thriving career in marketing, but she felt unfulfilled. She started volunteering for a local nonprofit organization in her spare time. Her passion for giving back grew, and she eventually left her corporate job to work full-time for the nonprofit. Her unconventional career shift not only brought her happiness but also made a significant impact on her community.

These stories remind us that success doesn't always follow a traditional path. By listening to their hearts, taking risks, and pursuing their passions, these individuals found fulfillment and happiness in unconventional ways. Their journeys inspire us to embrace

our own unique paths to success in our
modern world.

Chapter 7: The Joy of Giving

In our modern lives, the act of giving is a source of profound joy and fulfillment. This chapter explores the simple yet powerful concept of giving and its impact on our personal well-being.

The Gift of Giving

Imagine the joy of making someone smile. Giving is about sharing your time, resources, or kindness with others without expecting anything in return.

Modern Acts of Kindness

In our fast-paced world, small acts of kindness can make a big difference. Whether it's helping a neighbor, donating to a charity, or simply offering a listening ear, these acts of giving create a positive ripple effect.

Boosting Happiness

Giving isn't just beneficial for the recipients; it's also a source of happiness for the giver. Research shows that acts of kindness release "feel-good" chemicals in the brain, leading to increased well-being.

Strengthening Connections

Giving strengthens our connections with others. It fosters a sense of community and deepens our relationships. When we give, we create bonds of trust and empathy.

Creating Purpose

Giving can give life purpose and meaning. Knowing that your actions positively impact others can provide a sense of fulfillment that goes beyond personal gain.

The Modern Giving Landscape

In today's digital age, opportunities to give abound. You can support causes online, volunteer virtually, or join local community initiatives. Giving has never been more accessible.

The Journey Ahead

In the chapters that follow, we'll explore practical ways to incorporate giving into your life and share stories of individuals who've found immense joy in giving. Remember, the act of giving is a simple yet powerful way to enrich your life and make a positive impact on the world in our modern age.

The Joy of Giving

In our modern lives, the act of giving is a source of profound joy and fulfillment. This chapter explores the simple yet powerful concept of giving and its impact on our personal well-being.

The Gift of Giving

Imagine the joy of making someone smile. Giving is about sharing your time, resources, or kindness with others without expecting anything in return.

Modern Acts of Kindness

In our fast-paced world, small acts of kindness can make a big difference. Whether it's helping a neighbor, donating to a charity, or simply offering a listening ear, these acts of giving create a positive ripple effect.

Boosting Happiness

Giving isn't just beneficial for the recipients; it's also a source of happiness for the giver. Research shows that acts of kindness release "feel-good" chemicals in the brain, leading to increased well-being.

Strengthening Connections

Giving strengthens our connections with others. It fosters a sense of community and deepens our relationships. When we give, we create bonds of trust and empathy.

Creating Purpose

Giving can give life purpose and meaning. Knowing that your actions positively impact others can provide a sense of fulfillment that goes beyond personal gain.

The Modern Giving Landscape

In today's digital age, opportunities to give abound. You can support causes online, volunteer virtually, or join local community initiatives. Giving has never been more accessible.

The Journey Ahead

Remember, the act of giving is a simple yet powerful way to enrich your life and make a positive impact on the world in our modern age.

Finding Happiness Through Giving

In our modern lives, volunteerism and philanthropy are avenues that can lead to profound happiness. This chapter encourages readers to explore these paths and discover the joy of giving.

The Call to Give

Deep inside, many of us have a longing to make a difference. Volunteering and philanthropy are ways to answer that call and find happiness in the process.

The Power of Connection

When you volunteer or give to a cause you're passionate about, you connect with others who share your values. These connections can lead to meaningful relationships and a sense of belonging.

The Joy of Contribution

Contributing to a cause you care about, whether through your time, skills, or resources, can bring immense satisfaction. Knowing that you're making a positive impact is a source of happiness.

Creating Lasting Memories

Volunteer experiences and acts of philanthropy often create lasting memories. These are moments of fulfillment and happiness that stay with you for a lifetime.

The Modern Way to Give

In our digital age, finding volunteer opportunities and causes to support is easier than ever. You can browse online platforms, join virtual volunteering efforts, or donate to charities with a few clicks.

Start Small, Dream Big

You don't need to commit all your time or resources to make a difference. Start small, and gradually increase your involvement as you discover the joy of giving.

The Journey Ahead

Remember, the path to happiness often leads through the act of giving in our modern world.

Chapter 8: Financial Freedom vs. Material Wealth

In our modern lives, the concepts of financial freedom and material wealth often intertwine, but they aren't the same. This chapter explores the differences between the two and their relevance in our personal lives.

Material Wealth: The What

Material wealth refers to the possessions and assets we accumulate, such as money, property, and possessions. It's about having more "stuff" and often equated with success.

Financial Freedom: The How

Financial freedom, on the other hand, is about how you manage your resources. It's the ability to make choices without being constrained by financial worries. It means having control over your finances rather than your finances controlling you.

Modern Dilemma

In our consumer-driven world, there's immense pressure to accumulate material wealth. However, it's crucial to recognize that true wealth isn't just about having more things.

The Quest for Balance

Striving for financial freedom means making wise financial decisions, like saving, investing, and managing debt. It's about finding a balance between enjoying material comforts and securing your financial future.

Material Wealth as a Means

Material wealth can be a means to achieve financial freedom, but it's not the only path. Financial freedom can be achieved through careful financial planning, living within your means, and making intentional choices.

The Choice Is Yours

Ultimately, the choice between pursuing material wealth or financial freedom is a personal one. It's about defining what wealth means to you and how you want to live your life in our modern world.

The Journey Ahead

In the chapters that follow, we'll delve deeper into strategies for achieving financial freedom and explore how it can lead to a more fulfilling life. Whether you prioritize material wealth or financial freedom, the key is to align your choices with your values and goals.

Strategies for Financial Independence and Balance

In our modern lives, achieving financial independence while maintaining balance is a worthy goal. This chapter presents strategies to help you navigate your journey toward financial freedom and a more balanced life.

Define Your Goals

Start by defining your financial goals. What does financial independence mean to you? Do you want to retire early, travel more, or pursue a passion project? Knowing your goals provides direction.

Create a Budget

Establish a budget that outlines your income and expenses. This helps you understand where your money goes and where you can make adjustments to achieve your goals.

Reduce Debt

Work on reducing high-interest debts, such as credit card balances and loans. Reducing debt lowers financial stress and frees up resources for saving and investing.

Build an Emergency Fund

Create an emergency fund to cover unexpected expenses like medical bills or car repairs. This fund provides a safety net and prevents you from dipping into long-term savings.

Invest Wisely

Explore investment options that align with your goals and risk tolerance. Diversify your investments to spread risk and potentially increase returns over time.

Automate Savings

Set up automatic transfers to your savings and retirement accounts. This ensures that you consistently save and invest, even when life gets busy.

Live Within Your Means

Avoid lifestyle inflation. As your income grows, resist the urge to spend more. Instead, continue to save and invest the additional income.

Seek Financial Advice

Consider consulting a financial advisor or planner for personalized guidance. They can help you create a tailored strategy to achieve your financial goals.

Practice Self-Care

Remember that balance is key. Allocate time and resources to self-care, hobbies, and spending quality moments with loved ones.

Regularly Review Progress

Periodically assess your financial situation and adjust your strategy as needed. Celebrate milestones and stay committed to your journey.

The Journey Ahead

Remember, financial freedom is not just about money; it's about aligning your finances with your values and aspirations.

Chapter 9: Embracing the Journey

In our modern lives, the journey toward financial independence and a balanced life is a meaningful one. This chapter encourages you to embrace the path you're on and find fulfillment in the journey itself.

The Beauty of the Journey

Often, we're so focused on reaching our goals that we forget to appreciate the journey. Each step you take toward financial independence is an opportunity for growth and learning.

Small Wins Matter

Celebrate the small victories along the way. Whether it's paying off a credit card or increasing your savings, these achievements are steps toward your larger goals.

Adapt and Adjust

Life is full of surprises, and your financial journey may have twists and turns. Be adaptable and willing to adjust your plans when necessary. Flexibility is a valuable asset.

The Importance of Balance

While financial goals are important, don't forget to balance your life. Allocate time for hobbies, relaxation, and meaningful connections with others.

Continual Learning

The world of finance is always evolving. Keep learning and staying informed about new opportunities and strategies to improve your financial well-being.

Gratitude and Contentment

Practice gratitude for what you have today. Contentment with your current situation can bring a sense of peace and happiness on your journey.

The Journey's End Is Just the Beginning

Remember, achieving financial independence isn't the end of the road; it's the beginning of a new chapter. Your journey continues as you explore how to make the most of your newfound freedom.

The Journey Ahead

As you move forward in the chapters to come, keep in mind that the journey itself is a significant part of your life. Embrace it, savor it, and find fulfillment in every step you take on the path toward financial independence and balance in our modern world.

Living in the Present and Savoring Small Pleasures

In our modern lives, the present often slips away as we chase future goals. This chapter highlights the importance of living in the moment and finding joy in life's small pleasures.

The Rush of Modern Life

Our fast-paced world keeps us constantly on the move, planning for the future. It's easy to forget the beauty of the present moment.

The Gift of Now

The present is a gift. It's where you experience life fully, where small moments of happiness are waiting to be discovered.

Finding Joy in Simplicity

Happiness doesn't always come from grand achievements. It often hides in simple pleasures like a warm cup of tea, a smile from a friend, or a walk in nature.

The Power of Mindfulness

Practice mindfulness by paying attention to the here and now. Engage your senses in the present moment, whether it's savoring a meal, feeling the warmth of the sun, or listening to soothing music.

Gratitude for Today

Count your blessings and express gratitude for what you have right now. Gratitude can transform ordinary moments into extraordinary ones.

Balancing Goals and Presence

While it's important to plan for the future, striking a balance between future aspirations and present awareness is key to a fulfilling life.

The Journey Ahead

Remember, the richness of life unfolds in the moments you cherish in our modern world.

Mindfulness and Gratitude

In our modern lives, practicing mindfulness and gratitude can help us savor our experiences and find joy in everyday moments. This chapter offers simple practices to incorporate into your life.

Understanding Mindfulness

Mindfulness means being fully present in the moment, without judgment. It's about paying attention to your thoughts, feelings, and surroundings.

Practice Mindful Breathing

Take a few minutes each day to focus on your breath. Breathe in slowly and deeply, then exhale. Pay attention to the sensation of your breath. This practice calms the mind and anchors you in the present.

Engage Your Senses

When you eat, really taste your food. When you walk, notice the sensation of each step. Engaging your senses brings you into the moment.

Mindful Listening

When someone speaks to you, listen with your full attention. Avoid thinking about your response or distractions. Truly hear what they're saying.

Gratitude: The Key to Joy

Gratitude is about appreciating what you have. Each day, write down a few things you're thankful for. It can be as simple as a sunny day or a kind gesture from a friend.

Count Your Blessings

Regularly reflect on the positive aspects of your life. Take a moment to think about the good things that surround you. This practice shifts your focus to what's going well.

Gratitude Journaling

Keep a journal where you record moments of gratitude. Write down the things that make you feel thankful. Over time, this practice enhances your sense of contentment.

Modern Challenges, Timeless Practices

In our modern world filled with distractions, mindfulness and gratitude practices offer a way to connect with the present and find happiness in the simplest of moments. Incorporate these practices into your daily routine to savor your experiences and lead a more fulfilling life.

Chapter 10: The Path to True Wealth

In our modern lives, the pursuit of true wealth is a quest for genuine richness and fulfillment. This chapter explores the path to true wealth and its relevance in our personal journeys.

Beyond Material Riches

True wealth extends far beyond material possessions. It's about finding richness in life's experiences, connections, and personal growth.

Defining True Wealth

Each person's definition of true wealth is unique. It may involve meaningful relationships, personal well-being, purposeful work, or a sense of inner peace.

Modern Temptations

In a world that often equates wealth with money and possessions, it's easy to lose sight of what truly matters. True wealth lies in aligning your life with your values.

Pursuit of Balance

The path to true wealth involves finding balance between your material goals and your inner aspirations. It's about nurturing your soul as well as your bank account.

Prioritizing Happiness

Happiness is a fundamental aspect of true wealth. Prioritizing your well-being and joy leads to a richer and more fulfilling life.

The Journey Ahead

As you continue reading, you'll explore how to align your life with true wealth.

Remember, the path to true wealth is a personal journey that encompasses all aspects of your life.

Reevaluating Our Pursuit of Wealth

In our modern lives, the pursuit of true wealth goes beyond the accumulation of material possessions. This chapter underscores the need to reassess our chase for wealth and emphasizes the relevance of true wealth in our personal journeys.

Key Takeaways:

True Wealth Is Multifaceted:
True wealth encompasses more than just financial prosperity. It involves meaningful experiences, deep connections, personal growth, and inner contentment.

Unique Definitions:
Every individual defines true wealth in their own way. It may include happiness, fulfilling relationships, purposeful work, or inner peace. There is no one-size-fits-all definition.

Modern Distractions:

In a society that often equates wealth solely with monetary success, it's easy to lose sight of what truly matters in life. Reevaluating our priorities can lead to a more fulfilling existence.

Balancing Act:

Achieving true wealth involves finding equilibrium between material pursuits and inner aspirations. It's about nurturing both our financial well-being and our personal growth.

Prioritizing Happiness:

Happiness is a core component of true wealth. By prioritizing our well-being and joy, we can access a richer, more meaningful life.

This chapter encourages readers to reconsider their pursuit of wealth and explore the path to true wealth, a journey that is unique to each individual. It reminds us that the pursuit of genuine richness involves all aspects of our lives and calls us to align our actions with our values in our modern world.

Embracing the Journey to True Wealth

As we conclude this chapter on the pursuit of true wealth, it's crucial to encourage readers to embark on a journey toward a more fulfilling, purpose-driven life. The path to true wealth is not just a concept; it's an invitation to transform the way we live and find meaning in our modern world.

Your Personal Journey

Your journey to true wealth is a unique adventure. It starts with introspection and an honest assessment of what truly matters to you. Take the time to define your own version of true wealth.

Reassessing Priorities

Pause and reassess your priorities. Are you placing too much emphasis on material possessions? Are you neglecting your well-being, relationships, or passions? Use this chapter as a catalyst for change.

Taking Small Steps

Remember, the journey doesn't require a radical overhaul of your life. Small, intentional steps can lead to profound shifts. It might involve spending more quality time with loved ones, pursuing a hobby, or reevaluating your career choices.

Seeking Inspiration

Draw inspiration from the stories of those who have found true wealth in various ways. These stories serve as beacons of possibility, reminding us that richness can be discovered in unexpected places.

Living with Purpose

Ultimately, the pursuit of true wealth is about living a life of purpose and meaning.

It's about aligning your actions with your values, finding joy in the present moment, and prioritizing the well-being of yourself and those around you.

The Ongoing Journey

Your journey to true wealth is not a one-time endeavor but an ongoing exploration. As you move forward, reflect on your progress, adjust your course when needed, and cherish the richness of every moment.

In this chapter, we've explored the need to reevaluate our pursuit of wealth and emphasized the relevance of true wealth in our personal journeys. Now, it's your turn to embrace this journey, discover your own path to true wealth, and embark on a life that's truly fulfilling and purpose-driven in our modern world.

Conclusion: The Riches of Being Poor

As we conclude this chapter on the need to reassess our pursuit of wealth and emphasize the relevance of true wealth in our personal journeys, let's reflect on the paradox of finding riches in simplicity, contentment, and living aligned with our values.

True Richness

In our modern world, the pursuit of wealth often takes center stage. But true richness can be discovered in the simplicity of life, even when faced with limited material wealth.

Simplicity as a Choice

Being "poor" in material wealth can be a deliberate choice to live with less. It's an opportunity to declutter your life from excessive consumption and find richness in what truly matters.

Experiences Over Possessions

Without the burden of material possessions, you can focus on experiences that enrich your life. Time spent with loved ones, personal growth, and pursuing your passions become valuable treasures.

Freedom from Financial Stress

A simpler life often means fewer financial obligations. This freedom from debt and overspending can lead to reduced stress and greater peace of mind.

The Richness of Contentment

Being content with what you have and practicing gratitude can bring a sense of richness to your daily life. It's about appreciating the small pleasures and finding joy in the present moment.

Embracing the Paradox

The riches of being "poor" lie in the paradox of finding fulfillment through simplicity. It's about prioritizing what truly matters and living a life aligned with your values.

Your Unique Path

Remember, your path to true wealth may not always follow the conventional route. It may involve reevaluating your priorities, simplifying your life, and embracing contentment. This chapter invites you to explore this path and discover the riches of being "poor" in the context of our modern world.

Embracing a Simpler, More Purposeful Existence

As we wrap up this chapter on the need to reassess our pursuit of wealth and highlight the significance of true wealth in our personal journeys, I invite you, the reader, to reflect on your own values and priorities.

Your Unique Journey

Your life is a unique journey, and the pursuit of true wealth is a personal quest. Take a moment to consider what truly matters to you in our modern world.

Reflecting on Values

What are your core values? What brings you joy and fulfillment? What do you cherish most in life? These reflections can guide you toward a richer, more purposeful existence.

Simplifying Your Path

Consider simplifying your life by letting go of excess and embracing what aligns with your values. It might involve decluttering your possessions, reevaluating your commitments, or making space for meaningful experiences.

Prioritizing What Matters

True wealth often lies in prioritizing what truly matters—your well-being, relationships, personal growth, and contentment. Aligning your actions with your values can lead to a more fulfilling life.

Why You Should Be Poor (But Not Really)

In our whirlwind tour through the world of wealth, we've discovered a secret worth sharing: why you should be poor. But hold on, don't go selling your stuff just yet! Here's the scoop, with a sprinkle of humor:

Embrace the Simple Life: Being poor (in stuff, not in spirit) can mean a simpler, less cluttered life. Just think, fewer things to dust!

Collect Experiences, Not Junk: Instead of amassing stuff, collect memories and experiences. They don't take up closet space and are way more fun to look back on.

Be Debt-Free and Worry-Light: Less stuff often means fewer bills and less stress. Being poor in debt is a badge of honor.

Value What Matters: In the grand scheme of things, stuff isn't that important. Friends, family, and good vibes—now those are treasures!

The Richness of Contentment: Being content with what you have is like having a superpower. You're immune to the "I need more stuff" bug.

Unleash Your Inner Zen Master: Decluttering can be oddly satisfying. Plus, you'll discover corners of your home you forgot existed.

It's All About Balance: Okay, okay, you don't have to go full minimalist. Keep some stuff if it sparks joy, as the organizing gurus say.

So, why should you be poor? Because in our modern world, true wealth isn't about the size of your TV or the make of your car. It's about embracing a simpler, more purposeful life, where the richest treasures are the ones that money can't buy. So, be "poor" in possessions but rich in experiences, contentment, and laughter. It's the kind of "poor" that's secretly a jackpot.